Highly Productive Remote Work

Books by Darius Foroux

Win Your Inner Battles (2016)

How To Go From Procrastinate Hero to Procrastinate Zero (2016)

THINK STRAIGHT (2017)

Do It Today (2018)

The Road To Better Habits (2019)

What It Takes To Be Free (2019)

Courses by Darius Foroux

Procrastinate Zero 2

Effective Writing

Real Influence

How To Create Your Dream Career

Work First

Highly Productive Remote Work

A Pragmatic Guide

by

DARIUS FOROUX

Table Of Contents

Introduction

Remote work is my favorite type of work. Every knowledge worker in the world should work more from home. In my 10 years of experience with remote work, I can share that it has the following benefits:

1. **Better output:** When you work in an office, you're constantly dealing with distractions. If there's one enemy of good work, it's distractions. People often complain about having a lack of focus. They think something is wrong with them. That's false. You're fine. The place that you're working at is likely not.

2. **Higher work satisfaction:** Working from home or remotely from any other location gives you more freedom and control over your life. That leads to a better work experience.

3. **More time:** You don't have the hassle of waking up early, getting ready for work, rushing, and commuting to work. Think about it, how much time do you waste on those processes? When I worked at an IT research firm in London, I woke up at 6.30 AM and I was in the office around 8.45 AM, sometimes later if the train was delayed. That's up to 2.5 hours! I'm not even calculating the time it takes to get back from work.

But remote work is not easy. It requires a lot of effort to do it well. When you work at home, you're your own boss. That means you must manage yourself. If you're self-employed, you know how difficult that is.

As I'm writing this introduction, the world is in the midst of the COVID-19 crisis. Nearly all companies in the world are shut down. Everyone who can work at home is working at home. For most workers, this is a new experience. They are now all of a sudden alone. They need to manage their own time, energy, and focus. In my experience, there are two important aspects to highly productive remote work:

1. **Adopting a "work first" mindset:** Remote work requires a different mindset. You need to be more self-reliant, proactive, and emotionally centered.

2. **Apply the right productivity strategies:** Getting work done is actually very simple. There are only a few productivity strategies that you need to improve your output from home.

To help you improve both aspects, I've divided this book into two parts. Part I shows you how to shift your mindset. With the right mindset, you make sure that you're getting the most out of your time at home. You also make sure you're not distracted by inner disturbances. You might not have the usual office distractions around you, but you still have to deal with other things that distract you. Often, those distractions come from within.

Part II is a summary of the best productivity strategies I've come across in my career. I'm only sharing the most useful strategies with you. You can use these tips instantly to get more done. But here's the thing: Part II doesn't work if you don't adopt the "work first" mindset we cover in Part I. I'm going to talk about the importance of that mindset later. For now, I want to share the most important idea for everyone who works remotely. Make this Teddy Roosevelt quote your motto:

"Do what you can, where you are, with what you have."

Whether you're reading this book during a crisis or not, remote work is about the willingness to do whatever you can, where you are, with what you have. I love that.

Life is far from perfect. We all wish that we have a huge home office, a first-rate ergonomic chair, the latest monitor, the fastest computer, and so forth. But for most of us, we just have to make the best of what we have. That doesn't mean you shouldn't aim high and set goals to buy a bigger house.

I started my blog from my bedroom at my parents' house. At the time, I had just moved back from London. I didn't see this coming, but I had a sense that I needed to take charge of my career. I had a vision to work from home and earn a living with nothing more than a laptop. In today's world, that's a real possibility. In fact, I'm the perfect example. That little blog turned into an online business that generates six-figures a year. While the money is great, the freedom is more important. Ultimately, remote work is the vehicle that I used to get that freedom. We all have access to the tools and opportunities to do great work from any place in the world. All you need is a laptop and an internet connection.

What Highly Productive Remote Work Is About

This book shows you how to be highly productive no matter where you work. You can turn your home, hotel room, bedroom, guest room, or any other private space into your primary workspace. While the tips that I share in this book will work from any place, I don't recommend working from a coffee shop or shared office space. At least, don't make that your default. It might work for Malcolm Gladwell—who apparently does his best writing from coffee shops—but it will likely not work for you and me. We're creatures of habit. We need some form of routine and consistency. Now, it doesn't matter what that looks like. Simply work with what you have. Working from my bedroom wasn't ideal but I still did it. It was the only space I had at the time.

And I made sure I was highly productive no matter what. That's what this book is about. It will help you become someone like Teddy Roosevelt. You will be productive no matter what your circumstances are. This book contains a collection of articles that I handpicked to help you get more clarity in life. I've been writing about remote work and productivity since 2015. And I've rewritten many of the articles to turn them into a book form. I also added extra content that I never published before. The content of this book forms a system that shows you how to get things done from home, or any other place in the world. My goal is to share these ideas with you in one place, so you don't have to spend hours browsing the web or reading multiple books.

When you adopt the ideas, strategies, and habits that I write about in this book, you can immediately take on any work-related challenge that life throws at you. You no longer wish that you had a perfect office or the best resources in the world, you will be highly productive with what you have.

While the biggest part of the world is wasting their time on useless activities, you're here, reading this book. That already means you have a positive outlook on life. It only goes up from here Let's get started, my friend.

-Darius

March 21, 2020

Leeuwarden, The Netherlands.

PART I

MINDSET

"Don't think. Thinking is the enemy of creativity. It's self-con-scious, and anything self-conscious is lousy. You can't try to do things. You simply must do things."

— Ray Bradbury

The Work First Mindset

The most important thing that I've done for my career is to adopt what I call a "work first" mindset. About five years ago, I was tired of the ups and downs of my career. One day I was productive, the other day I was not. I tried a bunch of useless tips and tactics you read about on mainstream sites. Nothing worked for me. But through reading the biographies people who I looked up to, I learned that every single one of those folks had this "work first" mindset.

One of my favorite books is Daily Rituals by Mason Curry. In that book, you can read about the rituals of 161 inspirational artists, leaders, writers, scientists, and other creators.

I noticed that all of these people designed their days around their work. That doesn't mean other things are not important. It just means that you're committed to getting your work done no matter what. We all know that this is true. Think about that important deadline you had to make no matter what. Think about the time you had to step in when your co-worker was sick.

When the stakes are high, we always get things done. Did it matter what outfit you wore? Did it matter where you worked? Of course not! What matters is that you had a "work first" mindset during those times.

You can wear whatever you want, you can work from the couch, you can work at 2 AM or 6 PM, on the toilet, using any type of app you like. Practically speaking, a "work first" mindset means that you plan your day around your work. Your work literally comes first. And that looks different for every single person.

For me, it's simple. I wake up without an alarm, have some coffee, and start writing. Only after I've done my writing, I move on to the practical things of life. But as you and I both know, life is complex. You might have a demanding job or a kid that you need to take care of. Everyone has their own reasons they can't prioritize their work. That's okay.

Sometimes I get emails from people who try to explain their busy lives to me. "But you don't understand! I have all these things I have to do!" We *all* have things, so what? People who think their life is harder than other people don't get it. Life is hard for everyone. Complaining makes it only harder. What matters is that we make our work a priority. Why? Because work is important. It's the foundation of a functioning human society. Without work, everything would collapse.

So I never understand why people don't take their careers seriously. We can't take our career and work seriously enough. That doesn't mean you should become a workaholic. Somehow people make all kinds of odd assumptions. They assume that someone who takes something seriously is taking things to an extreme.

"Work first" is a philosophy. The basic idea is that you take your work seriously. It's a way of life. And you can apply it to different things. In fact, I also have a "family first" mindset. Who said you can't combine things in life? You see? That's another false assumption. As you're reading this book, I challenge you to drop every single assumption that you have.

I still remember the moment I dropped my assumptions. It was 2014 and I was talking to a hiring manager at Gartner, named Stella. I should probably message her to thank her. We had a normal job interview call and during the conversation, I asked her to be open with me. If she had any feedback, I preferred that she gave it to me straight up. That's what she did. "You're making a lot of assumptions." It was like a whole new world opened to me. I was making assumptions about everything! The way I see it, I never learned anything deeply until I stopped making assumptions.

We all have these made-up beliefs in our minds. Where does it all come from? Take the "work first" mindset. When I share it with people I work with, nearly all of them assume that you must be a workaholic. "So are you saying that your work is the most important thing in your life?" No. That's not what I'm saying. I simply make sure I get my work done every day before I turn on Netflix. That's what it is.

And I hold myself accountable. I do my job every day. But I don't do it ALL day. You see? In fact, I'm probably working fewer hours than you. On average, I work 4.5 hours a day. And yet, most people consider me a highly productive person. Why? I credit the majority of my output to my mindset. This is a mindset that I adopted. I wasn't born this way. How do you change your mindset? Let's talk about that in the next chapter.

How To Change Your Mindset

"I'm bored." When's the last time you said that? I bet not too long ago. If you give me 4 minutes, I'll tell you why that's a sign of a bad mindset.

In the past, I always looked at other people for answers. When you're little, your schoolteachers tell you what to do every day. That's the system at primary school, high school, college, and university. It's always one person who tells a group what to do. What does that do to people? School systems train us to be passive. And after we get out of school, nothing really changes. When I had my first job, I listened to my boss about what to do. And when I started my first business with my dad, I looked at him for answers.

Now, you might think that this is a matter of experience. That's the most obvious idea. We think: *"When I'm junior, I take orders. When I'm senior, I give orders."* That's about the worst mindset you can have because it's too passive. Instead, it's much more beneficial for our career to adopt the "work first" mindset. What's the difference between a passive and a "work first" mindset? And how do we even form a "work first" mindset? I have a three-step-process that I've used to transform my own mindset.

Step 1: Acknowledge that a passive mindset is bad

So when I talk about being bored, I'm not talking about being bored in a good way. Sometimes the best ideas come to us when we're fully relaxed. That's good. For the sake of this chapter, I'm talking about when we say I'm bored in an *"I have no idea what I'm doing"* type of way. Do you recognize that feeling? It's a sense of aimlessness.

Now, to a degree, no one knows what they are doing. The difference is that when you're always bored with life, you're not *trying*. And people who don't try are losers. You know why? Life is fascinating—but you must *try* to experience it. There's nothing cool about not having your shit together. You can't go through life as a passenger.

At some point, you must take over the wheel and decide where you're going next. That's the difference between people who have a "work first" mindset and people with a passive mindset. The former owns his destiny. The latter leaves it up to others.

Step 2: Commit to learning

The Stoic philosopher Seneca put it best in On the Shortness of Life: "If you apply yourself to study you will avoid all boredom with life, you will not long for night because you are sick of daylight, you will be neither a burden to yourself nor useless to others, you will attract many to become your friends and the finest people will flock about you."

That's why I believe a "work first" mindset has nothing to do with experience. I know interns who are more curious and ask more questions than most senior managers. But having a "work first" mindset has nothing to do with age or experience. For example, an insurance consultant in his sixties—who I work with—is as curious as an intern. He's enthusiastic about everything you talk to him about.

The other day I visited a printing company with my brother. The owner, a third-generation business owner, took over the business from his father years ago. He gave us a full tour and showed us the old printing presses they used, etc. My brother and I were genuinely interested.

The printing press, developed by Johannes Gutenberg, is the greatest invention for human progress. Without books, we wouldn't be where we are today. That's fascinating to me. The owner said, "I've never met anyone who actually asked about *how* we print our books, magazines, flyers, etc." Not many people commit to learning. That's why so many people are always bored. That shouldn't be a surprise to you by now.

Step 3: Start creating value

If you apply step 2, creating value becomes easy. When you're curious and ask questions, you learn. And when you learn, you will have more knowledge and ideas. When you have ideas, you can use them to improve your life, work, business, etc. That's the logic behind the "work first" mindset. The fact that you prioritize your work is actually a side effect. You're so passionate about your work that you take it seriously. You want to create value every single day. Why? Because that's your job.

When it comes to adopting a "work first" mindset; more knowledge will not help you—only action will. People with a passive mindset think that's common sense. They're quick to think they already know things. But as you and I both know; it's not about what you know, it's about what you do.

The most important thing is that we commit to learning. If you stay assertive and try to create value in life and business, you always have something to do. Plus, you keep making progress. And making daily progress (no matter how little) is the sure sign that you have a "work first" mindset. In the following chapters, we are going to dig deeper into the "work first" mindset. Every chapter covers an important principle of this mindset. If you apply all the following principles, you end up with a "work first" mindset.

Manage Your Energy

When I'm tired and low on energy, even the best things in life don't bring me joy. I never understood this for years. I regularly kept asking myself "Why am I not enjoying my work today?" It's because I was low on energy on those days. Looking back, I don't understand why I didn't get this earlier. It's so obvious. Energy is *everything*. It matters more than status, power, and even money. Jerry Seinfeld, who has all those things, said the following in an interview: *"I think money is great. But physical and mental energy is the greatest riches of human life."*

In the interview, he mentioned multiple times that he derived the most satisfaction from doing good work and feeling good. He said there's nothing better than a good day's work. But you need energy to do that. In fact, you need energy to do anything. When you're tired, you don't even want to get up from the couch: "It doesn't hurt to hold my pee for another hour, right?" I'm not a pee doctor, but I'm pretty sure it's not good for you.

Measuring Energy

The problem with energy is that we only miss it when we don't have it. The day I'm writing this, I've been feeling like my normal self. I had a cold for the past week. I had a headache, runny nose, and wasn't in the mood for anything. I lost focus and became pessimistic. I started questioning my work and felt an urge to get away from it all.

Fortunately, because I'm currently working on this topic, I caught myself slipping and reminded myself that I felt bad because of my low energy levels. Too often, we think something is wrong with our life or career while nothing might be wrong—you just need to recharge and everything will be fine. And that's what happened to me too. Personal energy is difficult to measure. Even scientists who researched energy admit that "Although energy is a concept that is implied in many motivational theories, it is hardly ever explicitly mentioned or researched."

But if you want to improve anything in life, you must measure it first. Otherwise, how do you know what improvement looks like? But because there's no single way to measure energy, it doesn't mean we can't attempt to measure our own energy.

The 3 Types Of Personal Energy

I've been doing my own research into personal energy. I've read books like The Power of Full Engagement and Flow. I've read scientific articles that I found on Google Scholar. But most importantly, I've been working as a trainer since 2015, and taught over 2,500 people to become more productive.

Here's what I've found: Our energy levels variate *a lot*. And we're not aware of its importance. That's the reason I started looking into personal energy in the first place. At some point, I realized that my energy level was far from consistent. Some days I felt great, energized, and excited. Other days I felt tired, down, and I wasn't in the mood for anything.

On top of that, there were periods, sometimes weeks or even months, I felt energized. But I also had weeks when I was low on energy. I realized that there's not one single measure of personal energy. I've found 3 types of energy. And if one is out of whack, your whole system takes a hit. They are:

1. **Mental Energy**—Your ability to concentrate, focus, work, pay attention, listen, etc.

2. **Physical Energy**—Your ability to perform physical tasks.

3. **Emotional Energy**—Your ability to show compassion to yourself and to others.

How can we improve every type of personal energy? Even though there are many different factors that influence our energy levels, I'm sharing one tip for improving each energy type.

1. Meditation Improves Mental Energy

There are many different types of meditation. My favorite is Mindfulness meditation. Research into the benefits of Mindfulness is vast. I don't need to mention them here. Thousands of years of practice and research have shown that meditation is an excellent tool for improving our focus and awareness.

And that's exactly what will give you more mental energy. When your thoughts are scattered and consume you, life sucks. It's like living in a world that always has foggy weather. Imagine what that would look like. You can't see clearly. You can only see what's right in front of you. On top of that, everything is grey. When you don't meditate, that's how you're living.

When you remove the fog, and let in the sunshine, you all of a sudden see how beautiful your world is. If you don't meditate, you probably think I'm full of shit. I'm with you. I used to make fun of people who meditate too. "Sitting still? Doing nothing? I might as well hug trees!" Just give it a try. And keep returning to it.

If you're meditating already and you're still low on energy, try another form of meditating. I also like walking and running meditation. Meditation is like working out, not everyone likes the same type of exercise.

2. Exercise Improves Physical Energy

Again, you don't need me to tell you that exercise will make you stronger. The problem is that most of us don't *make time* to do it. You and I both know that you have time to work out. One of my students who has two kids recently told me she used her busy life as an excuse for doing hard things: "It's soooo easy to tell yourself. I need to work, cook, clean, and to take care of the kids."

We've all been there. We say that we don't have the time. But why is it that we have time for watching two hours of tv every day? Why do we have 90 minutes a day for social media? The truth is that we make time and it's all about awareness. As my student realized: "The way I look at it now is that I'm working out before I'm going to turn on Netflix." Prioritize exercise, my friend. You've heard it thousands of times. But if you don't place it up there with sleeping, eating, and breathing, you'll never do it consistently.

3. Human Interaction Improves Emotional Energy

This is so important in today's society. In large cities, people are growing more emotionally apart while being so physically close to each other. Again, there's a lot of research about the impact of social interactions on our well-being.

We are inherently compassionate beings. We all have the capacity to care and to share. But if we're isolated, we can't do any of them. The more you close yourself off to other people, the worse you will feel. In today's world, people get upset so easily. We all have an ego and we're quick to identify ourselves as something. You know what that causes? Only more distance. If others want to do that, let them. But never let other people destroy your compassion.

I've been running a business with my family for 9 years. That has tested our relationships often, but it has also improved our compassion. I encourage everyone to care more for others. Call your co-worker or friend every once in a while (yes, even if they don't call you first). Spend time with people without a particular reason or agenda, simply for the sake of human interaction. And meet new people. That's something I also want to do more of. Human interaction gives us energy. Especially when we interact with other people who have a positive outlook on life.

Aim For Consistency

When I focus on the three things above, my energy levels are great. When my energy is low, I always return to meditation, exercise, and human interaction. If you're not feeling well, the solution is somewhere in those three things.

The most important thing to remember is that cultivating, managing, and boosting personal energy is complex. There is no exact way to boost your mood. But what I can tell you is that you can't neglect one of the three types of energy and expect to feel good. You might meditate and exercise, but if you live in isolation, you still miss the energy you get from social interactions. You need mental, physical, *and* emotional energy to feel good. And when you feel good, bad times will not hurt you that much. Plus, good times will feel even better. All of this is a recipe for a consistently good life. Start managing your energy and see it for yourself.

Be Ambitious In Your Work

What human traits predict career and life success? I've been curious about that question since I was 16. But at that age I didn't think ambition was important. That was also the time I became interested in personal development. I wanted to improve my life and become a better student, friend, son, and human being.

I *decided* to build a good life for myself and the people in my life. Now, 16 years later, I think that decision was probably the most important decision of my life. That was the day I embraced ambition. You see, building a good life and career is one of the most difficult things in life. To be honest, you have to be a little ignorant to believe you can succeed in life.

The Odds Are Against You

Unless you're born into wealth, all the odds are against you. Most people let life happen to them. Just look at the numbers. Depression is at an all-time high, obesity has become more common, people are sitting at home with burnouts, etc.

I can go on for a while. Life ain't pretty—we all know that. So what makes you think you'll be successful? Really. Think about it. Why do you even think you'll be successful? Here's the simple answer: If you don't start with believing in yourself, you'll never start at all. And if you don't start, there will be no success whatsoever. That's the power of ambition. To be clear, when I talk about success, I'm not talking about monetary success. I'm talking about living life on your terms. To have a job you love, to be surrounded by the people you love, and to have a positive outlook for the future. That's success—not having a lot of money, power, and status.

Belief + Effort

Albert-László Barabási, a professor at Northeastern University, and the author of The Formula, studied the laws of success. He found that ambition plays a major role in success. For example, Barabási's research shows that students don't excel because of the school they attend. Often, we assume that people who went to a university like Harvard become high achievers *because* of their education. We think that Ivy League graduates somehow get different training and that's what makes them successful in the long-term. That's a wrong assumption. In The Formula: The Universal Laws of Success, Barabási's writes:

"The single determinant of long-term success was derived from the best college a kid merely applied to, even if she didn't get in. Meaning that if she applied to Harvard, got rejected, and went to Northeastern, her success was on a par with that of Harvard graduates who matched her SATs and high school grades."

Put simply, *ambition* is what makes someone great, not the school they went to. Barabási's research backs up what Henry Ford said decades ago: *"Whether you think you can or think you can't, you're probably right."*

But you and I both know that we don't automatically become successful if we *believe* we will. Belief by itself is not enough. Your performance needs to back your beliefs; otherwise you'll never get any tangible results. Also, success remains complex. There are no blueprints or roadmaps that guarantee anything. I don't think success can be replicated. But that's not the point I'm making here.

Ambition: Always *Believe* You Can Do Something

That's my point. When I decided that I could make something out of my life, I purposefully worked on making that happen. And this is what most people don't get. Yes, belief by itself is useless. But here's the thing: **The people who *believe* they can achieve their goals are the ones who actually *do*.**

So make ambition your *default*. When you set a big goal for yourself, don't automatically think, "I can never do that." You have to be ambitious enough to actually set some big goals for yourself. Why would you settle for average?

My goal with blogging was to do this full time and not only as a part-time struggling writer. I wanted to make a *good* living. But when I started, I made about $500 in the first year. During that year, I thought to myself, "How on earth can I get comfortable if I'm not earning enough to pay my mortgage?"

But I had other streams of income and kept at it. Eventually, I started earning six figures with writing alone. Of course it wasn't that simple. I've been improving myself and investing in my skills for 16 years. But hey, you can't expect to get anything for free in life. It's simply the price we pay for accomplishment.

Just look back on anything you've achieved in your life. Remember the beginning of each school year? You didn't know anything about your new subjects. But eventually, you passed your exams and at the end of the ride got your degree.

Same thing with work. What did you know on your first day? Nothing, right? I remember the first day I started all my jobs and businesses. I knew nothing! But look at what you've learned since then. You can learn a lot in a short amount of time. You start at zero and make progress every day. That's how you will achieve your new goals too. But only if you *believe* you will.

Adopt These Traits

Your personality is defined by what you do, not by what you say. Highly effective people have certain personality traits that make them the way they are. Sometimes we look at a great person and think, "I can never be like that!" False. While we all have personality traits that seem to be part of our DNA, my experience is that your personality can be shaped more than you think. I've adopted personality traits that were contrary to my nature and culture.

I grew up in The Netherlands. My experience is that people here are generally unnecessarily contrarian and pessimistic. That's why less than 3% of my readers are Dutch. They don't like personal growth.

I was like that too. But when I started traveling a lot after I graduated, I changed my views. I was exposed to personal growth and adopted many traits of highly effective people—people that I met through work and life. But I also learned from reading about inspiring people. What follows is a list of 12 positive personality traits. I learned about these traits by studying effective people from all walks of life. By adopting these traits for ourselves, and acting accordingly, we can purposefully form our *own* unique personality.

1. **Capable**—There's no exception to this trait. I've never met effective, happy, or successful people who weren't capable. They take their life and work seriously. They do things with a purpose. And most importantly, they know what they are talking about.

2. **Curious**—Effective people avoid assumptions. This used to be my biggest pitfall. I made assumptions about everything. One of my co-workers once told it to me straight: Stop making so many assumptions! That's what I did. I decided to become curious instead. Effective people ask a lot of questions. That's how you avoid assumptions.

3. **Assertive**—People think you have to be nice. That's wrong. It's good to be polite, but you don't have to go out of your way to be nice all the time. Effective people think about themselves. But they don't sacrifice others. That's what assertiveness is about.

4. **Forgiving**—Holding grudges is the least effective thing you can do. So many people have destroyed relationships and group dynamics because of grudges. "How could that person do this to me!" You ask. Well, maybe that other person doesn't even know why! People do stupid things. Move on.

5. **Independent**—Effective people are not easily influenced by others. They *listen* to others. But they are independent thinkers. They are not easily swayed by outside events.

6. **Respectful**—You know how insecure people make subtle digs at you or other people? "You look so tired. What's going on?" That's one of those dirty remarks that's meant to make you feel bad. There are a lot of people who want to put you down, which automatically makes them feel better than you. Respectful people never do that. You can also disagree with people and still be respectful. Basically, effective people are the opposite of internet trolls.

7. **Truthful**—When you regularly tell lies (no matter how small they are), you will eventually get caught by your own web. Call me superstitious (or a "little-stitious," as Michael Scott, the character from The Office, once said), but I think lies will eventually catch up with you. That's why it's better to tell the truth. It's not always pretty, but at least it's not a lie.

8. **Precise**—It's hard to explain things in a few words. It requires thought and effort to be precise. That's why you see a lot of people talk endlessly. They don't know what to say, so they use a shotgun approach. They spray words and hope a few will hit the mark. To be precise, you want to be like a marksman. Every sentence serves a purpose.

9. **Fair**—People who say that fairness is an impossible concept are usually not fair people. There are universal principles of fairness. In summary, be straight with people and don't play favorites. Be consistent in the way you treat people. That's the fairest thing we can do. And yes, that seems impossible in practice because it goes against our nature sometimes. But effective people do a lot of things that go against nature. They do things that others don't do.

10. **Flexible**—Life is complex and full of change. To survive and thrive, one must adapt all the time. That's why effective people are highly flexible and fluid. If you give them a new idea that works better than their old one, they go with the new one. They don't care about their ego or not looking smart. They care about what *works*.

11. **Self-aware**—Knowing what you can and *can't be*, will make your life a lot easier. Too often, we're not aware of who we are. But to be effective, you must know who you are and what you're made of. And if you have weaknesses or make mistakes, self-awareness will help you become honest about it. There's nothing wrong with imperfection. In fact, if you're not imperfect, you're probably a robot.

12. **Optimistic**—Give effective people a challenge, and they'll think about a solution. Give them a bleak outlook, and they'll find things to be grateful for. In contrast, being pessimistic is the easiest thing in the world. Everyone can complain and say, "we can't do that." But it takes strength to say, "let's figure out a way to make it happen."

Your personality is not set in stone. You might have certain natural tendencies. But with the right mindset, you can adopt any one of the above personality traits. Which one(s) you want to adopt depends on your nature. But you can't go wrong with the positive traits. Remember that it's a *choice* to become a certain person. It's only a matter of time to change yourself. Because once you set your personality and act accordingly, you're no longer becoming a certain way; you simply *are* that way.

Rely On Yourself

In my twenties, I often found myself aimless in life. It seemed like every other week, I had no idea what to do next in my life and career. I had no certainty. Do you know how that feels? It's a feeling of unease. A random thought or event would trigger worry, and before I knew it, I felt confused. It could be anything.

Maybe I read something on the news about rising house prices, a potential recession, or increasing crime rates. Or, it could be co-workers that caused confusion with stories about so and so who lost his job and couldn't pay his mortgage. You know how people gossip and talk, right? "You wouldn't believe this!" That's what people say before they share some weird story that's not even relevant to you.

All these things can confuse you. And what do you do when you're confused? That's right, just like any other modern human being, you try to look for some answers on *Google*! And we all know what happens when we turn to Google. You either end up reading about some terminal disease, the end of the world, or the Illuminati. If it's not something negative, you'll end up on the Instagram pages of the happiest and beautiful people in the world. This only makes things worse.

Why do we do that to ourselves? Most of us have this tendency to turn to *others* for answers. We look at what our friends, family, co-workers, or fellow students to do, say, or think we should do. But you and I both know that the answers do not lie outside of us. We know good and well that we should not ask others what we should do—we must ask *ourselves.*In my twenties, I often found myself aimless in life. It seemed like every other week, I had no idea what to do next in my life and career. I had no certainty. Do you know how that feels? It's a feeling of unease. A random thought or event would trigger worry, and before I knew it, I felt confused. It could be anything.

Maybe I read something on the news about rising house prices, a potential recession, or increasing crime rates. Or, it could be co-workers that caused confusion with stories about so and so who lost his job and couldn't pay his mortgage. You know how people gossip and talk, right? "You wouldn't believe this!" That's what people say before they share some weird story that's not even relevant to you.

All these things can confuse you. And what do you do when you're confused? That's right, just like any other modern human being, you try to look for some answers on *Google*! And we all know what happens when we turn to Google. You either end up reading about some terminal disease, the end of the world, or the Illuminati. If it's not something negative, you'll end up on the Instagram pages of the happiest and beautiful people in the world. This only makes things worse.

Why do we do that to ourselves? Most of us have this tendency to turn to *others* for answers. We look at what our friends, family, co-workers, or fellow students to do, say, or think we should do. But you and I both know that the answers do not lie outside of us. We know good and well that we should not ask others what we should do—we must ask *ourselves*.

To Get More Certainty, Learn How To Fish

Have you heard of that proverb about giving a man fish vs. teaching him how to fish? *"Give a man a fish and you feed him for a day. Teach a man to fish and you feed him for a lifetime."* As a society, we're all hungry for fish, but we don't want to learn *how* to fish. We can't be bothered. We would rather have people feeding us instead of fetching our own food.

Why is that? There's nothing noble about holding up your hand. It's much nobler to take care of yourself, to be self-reliant, to work, to earn. Relying on yourself will also give you certainty. Now that I've spent years improving my skills, building a network, and running two businesses, other people don't confuse me with their shenanigans anymore. I'm inwardly focused. Externals don't bother me as much as they did in the past.

Self-Reliance Is Not The Same As Stubbornness

Somehow people assume that self-reliance is about doing everything by yourself, not working with others, and only caring about yourself. Honestly, that sounds more like narcissism to me. Self-reliance is nothing more than being self-sufficient. It means not *clinging* to people. It means not making life harder for others than it already is.

Remember: We can't do everything in life by ourselves. That's where self-awareness comes into play. When you're self-reliant and self-aware, you know what you can and can't do. You also know what you like and don't like. Without self-awareness, I would still be a stubborn idiot. And probably a lonely one too.

In today's world that's filled with opportunities, the more self-reliant and self-aware you are, the more certainty you will have. And when you have more certainty, you'll have more energy to work on what gives you inner satisfaction. If you know what you want, and know how to get it, you *will* get it. It's just a matter of time.

Deal With Anxiety Head-On

One of my friends recently experienced sudden bouts of anxiety. Since he knew I've been there too, he asked me: "How do you deal with anxiety?" That's a good question. In the past, I looked for ways to "get over" or "beat" anxiety. I was looking for a cure. After reading dozens of books and hundreds of articles on the subject, I've found the answer: Anxiety can't be cured. It must be *dealt* with.

Dealing with anxiety is an ongoing battle for most of us. It's not a game or tournament. It's not like you can beat anxiety once and be over with it forever. Too often, people say they have "beaten" anxiety. I don't buy that. The only way you can truly beat anxiety is if you hide from life's hardship.

Dealing with criticism, hate, and negativity

Last month, my articles were read by more than a million people. Naturally, my content also gets attention from people who *don't* like it. And some of those folks take the time to share their opinion. I have no problem with that. The internet is a free place and everyone can say what they want. Most people are civil about their criticism. But sometimes, I get hateful messages.

Most writers and content creators don't like that. Initially, I also didn't like it when people criticized my stuff. "If you don't like it, why read it?" Is what I told myself. But as I got these hateful messages more often, I saw an opportunity. When someone criticizes you, you feel disturbed and maybe even anxious. It's not a fun feeling. I'd rather read an email from a reader who made a big change to his or her life after reading an article.

Fortunately, that also happens. But I've also learned to like the hate. Why? Because it's training. You have to deal with it. Avoiding it is not an option to me. I recently read an article from an author who proudly said that his assistant scans his email for criticism and hate so he doesn't get to see it. I get that. It's not fun to read that stuff. But how can you develop a thick skin without exposing yourself to criticism?

Face it: Life's not easy

Look, my first response to almost everything that's uncomfortable in life is to avoid it. I don't want to read hate mail. I don't want to deal with annoying realtors when I'm looking for real estate. I don't want to market my book. I don't want to run when I'm tired. I want everyone to love my content. I want people to give me the best deals. I want everyone to buy my book by themselves. I want to be in shape and feel good without working at it.

But you and I both know that's not reality. The truth is that life's not easy. We're confronted with uncomfortable things all the time. And that causes a lot of anxiety.

- What if my business fails?

- What if no one likes me?

- What if he/she rejects me?

- What if I end up alone?

- What if I get ill?

- What if my family dies?

Realize this: Anxiety is normal. It's a part of *normal* life. When you try to avoid feeling anxious, you're not living. I always remind myself of that. When I feel anxiety, it means I'm doing something right. However, it becomes a problem when we're always anxious. And there's no magic solution to that either.

Dealing with anxiety is hard and will always be hard. Never say, "Why me?!" Say, "This IS me!"

A few things that help with anxiety

Changing your mindset will help a lot with dealing with anxiety. But you also need action to prevent anxiety from controlling your life. You don't want to just get "better" at dealing with it. No, you want to contain that sucker every single day. Here are a few things that will help:

- **Work out every day**—This helps you with physical and mental strength. The stronger you are, the more confident you'll feel.

- **Start your day with something that's uncomfortable**—Just because I publish a lot of articles people assume I always like to write. That's not the case. Writing is a hard and tedious practice. And I often want to avoid it. That's why I force myself to start the day with writing. When I worked in sales, I started my day with prospecting.

- **Journal about your anxiety**—Bring all your darkness to the surface. It cannot survive in the light.

You see, there's no other solution. You have to go *through* the anxiety. You have to confront that feeling in your stomach and say, "I'm not afraid of you." At some point, you realize it's just a feeling. It's powerless once you stop feeding it. Fear can't do anything but scare you. Ask yourself: Do you really want a silly feeling to hold you back from experiencing life to the fullest? I don't. How about you?

Learn To Let Go

A while back, I noticed that I became restless when I couldn't work out or go to the gym. I was so used to working out that I made it a part of my identity. I couldn't let go of it. Do you know what that feels like? It's the same when you can't stick to any one of your habits—good or bad.

Waking up early, reading, meditating, journaling, you name it. What happens if we can't stick to our good habits? We become restless. That's harmful behavior because you're not fully free. I mentioned the working out example to my friends recently, and every single one of them who worked out regularly could relate.

Let go

Whether you're attached to good or bad habits, you're being controlled by your urges. That's the bottom line here. If you don't do certain things you *oblige* yourself to do on a day, and feel bad about failing to do them, your emotions are in control.

One of my goals is to remain free from my desires and urges. I want to be okay with letting things go. We all desire certain things in life: we want to be healthy, to always look young, to be loved, to be wealthy, etc.

If we don't get those things, we become disappointed. We can't let go of the desire. There are also a lot of things in life we despise: we don't want to become overweight, ill, old, lazy, jobless; you name it. And we do everything to avoid what we hate.

Let go of all that stuff! All the desires and the aversions. This idea comes back in different philosophies. There's this quote from the Buddha that captures the idea well: "You can only lose what you cling to."

How to practice

Clinging to anything is not helpful. We've all experienced that when we clung to an idea, promise, goal, or loved one. We must let go. But how do you practice letting go? I came up with a simple exercise that helps to control your urges and habits. It looks like this:

- **Are you addicted to the gym?** A few times a year, decide not to go. Make that decision consciously. When you feel great, just say, "I'm not going this week because *I decide* to." Don't worry, you won't lose your strength or stamina. That only declines after 1-2 weeks.

- **Are you addicted to posting things on social media or on a blog?** BOOM! Get off for a week. The world will not end. People might miss you, but they will be fine. I've done this with publishing articles. Earlier this year, I stopped regularly publishing because I didn't want to cling to it. Nothing happened. I just picked it up when I came back.

- **Are you addicted to working in the evening?** Stop and hit the couch for a few evenings. You won't turn into a slouch. Just pick up your work the next day or week.

- **Are you reading every day?** Consciously decide to stop reading for a week. Take that time to do nothing. Let all the information you acquired brew in the back of your mind.

You get the idea. This exercise helps you to distance yourself from your habits. Because most of what we do comes from fear. We fear that we lose our job if we don't work enough. We fear losing people's interest if we don't post enough. We fear we lose our health if we don't work out. You and I both know that as long as we're driven by fear, we're not free.

True freedom means you're not attached to any habit or thing in life. Remember, we own nothing in life. No one said it better than Epictetus (Greek Stoic Philosopher) in The Good Life Handbook: "You cannot really lose anything because you don't own anything in the first place. Not the stuff you have, nor your spouse, nor your property. They are given to you to keep temporarily. So never say, "I have lost something." You just returned it. And how painful it is to admit this, the same is true for the people in our lives. Clinging to people we love will only suffocate them. No matter how you look at attachment and clinging to habits, objects, or people, it's something that you want to avoid.

When I reflect on the times in my life when I attached to things too much, it never ended well. In contrast, most good things in my life come from letting go. Once you learn to let go consistently, you will become free. That will not only improve your own life—but also the lives of people that surround you.

How To Break A Negative Thought Loop

Sometimes a small thing disturbs me and causes a negative thought loop. Somebody might say something that rubs me the wrong way. I might get a minor injury that prevents me from working out. Something at work might go wrong.

Do you know that feeling? Before you know it, you're questioning everything about your life, career, health, or relationship. You do everything to resist the situation. You try to fix it. You feel compelled to address the disturbance.

But here's the thing, you don't control the disturbance. That frustrates you even more. Now, you're getting sucked in by negative thoughts. At this point, something that started as a small annoyance became a big life problem. You feel like quitting your job or relationship. You feel like everything works against you. And that nothing is worth it. That's a negative thought loop. I've experienced that very often. And I bet you have too. Why do we experience this?

It's about control. We think life should be a certain way. In other words, we want everything to happen the way we want. And if it doesn't, we flip out. Negative thought loops often start when something comes to an end. Have you noticed that?

Filling The Void

Look, *everything* in life comes to an end. Your job, business, career, relationships, friendships, and so forth. And every time something comes to an end in our life, it's like a little death. Something dies and leaves a void inside us. This event by itself is neither good nor bad. It's the nature of life. We can turn endings into bad things by trying to replace the thing that left our life. For example, when a relationship ends, a lot of people try to fill the void by taking on more work.

I've done that as well. All the time and energy you spent on the relationship becomes free when it ends. And because you don't want to feel alone, you try to fill the void by working more. You want to set higher goals and do a better job. But that's only you escaping reality.

The truth is that endings suck. But it's also a natural part of life. We should not resist change. Some things, we can't replace in life. If you lose your job, you can't simply replace working by spending more time with your spouse. And yet, that's exactly what many of us do. We either lose our job or fail at work and we think, "Now I can at least spend more time with my family." You're trying to fill the void. But that takes too much energy. And when some minor thing causes a negative thought loop, it causes your foundation to shake. Why? Because your foundation was weak all this time.

Everything Has Its Place

You can't fill a relationship void with work or exercise. You can't fill a health void with alcohol or drugs. You can't fill a work void with spirituality. You need to catch yourself when you're trying to escape reality. And that's one of the hardest things in life. Too often, people live their entire life in denial. We can't let that happen. We need to look inward.

I can tell you from personal experience that's very hard. I always struggle when something in my life ends. My first response is always to find a replacement. But I've learned that everything has its place. You can't replace your friends with your boyfriend or girlfriend. You can't replace exercise with working more. You need to allocate the right amount of time and energy to all aspects of life.

Thousands of years of evolution has shown us that human beings have similar needs. We need safety, support, relationships, joy, perspective, and something useful to do with our time. That's true for every person. When you recognize that simple fact about life, it forces you to take a helicopter view. You need to elevate your perspective on your life.

When you're stuck in a negative thought cycle, you have zero perspective. You're consumed by your thoughts. You need to force yourself to look at life in general. Not just your current situation. Look at life's nature—it's about motion.

Letting Go To Break The Negative Thought Loop

Michael A. Singer, an entrepreneur who once ran a large software company, and the author of The Untethered Soul, summarized the concept of letting go well: *"It's pretty black-and-white. You either let go or you don't."*

He speaks from experience. Singer was prosecuted by the Department of Justice for securities fraud. During that time, he risked losing it all. Eventually, all charges against him were dropped and his name was cleared, but he let go of it way before that. In fact, he wrote The Untethered Soul *while* he was being prosecuted.

If a person who's facing the risk of losing it all can let go, you and I also can. People often come up with all kinds of excuses. They say it's easier said than done and that letting go is not easy. No one said it's easy to break a negative thought loop. We all have our own challenges and obstacles. Sometimes people try to convince others that they are really having a hard time. Honestly, no one cares. You let go for *yourself. So if you're stuck inside a negative thought loop, know that you only have two options:*

1. You continue and let it destroy you

2. You let go and move on

The choice is yours. And yes, it's that simple. Decide between those two options and see for yourself.

Stoic Wisdom From Marcus Aurelius

How does one live well? It's a question that our fellow human beings have been pondering for centuries. Out of that simple question, many philosophies and religions have been born. But no philosophy does a better job of explaining the ideas for living well in a practical way than Stoicism.

The Emperor-Philosopher Marcus Aurelius, once the most powerful man on earth, was also a practitioner of Stoicism. Marcus wrote a collection of thoughts, ideas, and rules for life in what was later published as Meditation. He wrote the things in that book for his own use. He was practicing the philosophy of Stoicism. I read that in The Inner Citadel by Pierre Hadot, a book that analyzes Meditations. In that book, I also read that Marcus had 3 rules for life that are found throughout Meditations.

Hadot identifies the 3 rules for life of Marcus Aurelius as the following concepts: (1) judgment (2) desire (3) impulse toward action. As I was reading The Inner Citadel, I had difficulty grasping what Hadot meant by those three concepts. He does not tell us what to do with this information. He only says that Marcus Aurelius's work was dominated by three rules that are based on judgment, desire, and an impulse toward action.

Because when I talk about "rules for life," I think about directives. I think about "do this" and "don't do that." I use these types of rules in my life all the time. I look at rules like shortcuts that make life simple. By this, I do not want to minimize the work of Hadot. In fact, I think his analysis of philosophy is the best that I have ever read. His conclusions about Stoicism and philosophy are spot on. And if you want to study Stoicism, I recommend Hadot's work. But it's not a light read—even for well-read people. That's why I sat down to translate the 3 rules for life of Marcus Aurelius, as found by Pierre Hadot, in plain English. Here they are (for every rule, I mention a Marcus Aurelius quote that explains the idea):

Rule 1: Aim for pure judgment of events

"Suppress the value-judgment (which you add), and the 'I've been hurt' is also suppressed. Suppress the 'I've been hurt,' and the harm is suppressed." (Book IV, 7)

We need to put that quote in context. Marcus realized that we make judgments about everything. But instead of making a pure judgment, we make value-judgments. We add a personal twist to our judgment. In the above example, Marcus talks about when something bad that happens to you. In that case, you can say, "So and so happened to me. *And that hurt me.*"

The last sentence is the value-judgment part. So when you drop that last part, you don't let the bad thing to make an impact on you. The event merely happened. *The end.*

Let's say you lose your job. What's worse? The actual event of losing your job? Or you, worrying that you will never find a new job. Of course, it's the last part—the worrying.

When you make a judgment like that and give meaning to events, you're not making a *pure* judgment. So remember to look at everything that happens to you for what it is. Did your partner cheat on you? Did you get ill? Did you lose money? Did people make fun of you? Stab you in the back? The events *themselves* can't hurt you if you don't let them. Hence, aim for pure judgments of events. Did something happen? Fine. Do something or move on.

Rule 2: Only desire what's inside your control

"Love only the event which comes upon us, and which is linked to us by Destiny." (Book VII, 57)

In his Meditations, Marcus continuously repeats to himself that most things in life are outside of his control. He realized that life is unpredictable. In 2000 years, nothing has changed about that. Shit happens to you all the time. Instead of resenting it or desiring a different life; work with what you *have* and turn it to something positive. We all know this piece of advice. "If life gives you lemons, make lemonade," so the overused platitude goes. Marcus takes it one step further. Instead of making the best of what happens to you, LOVE it.

He knew that most of the things we desire are outside of our control. Look at what you desire. More money? A social media following? A better job? A new car? Or maybe that your partner will always love you? That you always keep your friends?

He desired none of the above. He only desired *what's inside his control* or what happened to him. He had faith in something bigger than him. What happened to him happened for a reason. Most things in life that happen are not up to you, my friend. And Marcus realized that like no one else. Only desire what's inside your control.

Rule 3: Act according to the common good

"In the first place: nothing at random, and nothing unrelated to some goal or end. Second, don't relate your actions to anything except an end or goal which serves the human community." (Book XII, 20)

Remove impulses from your life. Make your actions purposeful and never waste your energy on nonsense. Have a goal. This is what Marcus is saying in the above quote. To many, it sounds like too much control. "OMG. This is OCD." That may be. If people want to waste their time on this earth let them. Marcus didn't care for those folks. And neither should you. We are here for a reason: To make things better.

And that's why so many people are drawn to the writings of Marcus Aurelius and other Stoics. They wanted to make the world a better place. I can't think of a more noble goal than that. It is now up to us to keep this philosophy alive. And you can only do that by putting these 3 rules for life in *practice*.

Stop Being So Distracted

There's this idea in Eastern and Western philosophy that we must learn how to enjoy the present moment without getting distracted by the past or future.

Ever since the invention of words, the human race has been lost in thought. We are constantly thinking, stressing, worrying, and being preoccupied with a force that seems outside of our control. That's why many of us search for refuge in philosophies that promise us inner calm. Stoicism, Mindfulness, Zen—most of us use the teachings to escape our thoughts.

We keep on treating the symptoms by using meditation apps, reading comfortable books and articles, getting rid of our devices, and trying the next solution that promises peace from ourselves. I'm guilty of this too. I'm always looking for new knowledge and information. At some point, I learned that more information is not the answer.

But what CAUSES this state of mind we are in? The answer is our excessive desire. There's an Epicurean saying that the stoic philosopher Seneca talks about in one of his letters: *"The life of a foolish man is fearful and unpleasant; it is swept totally away into the future."*

Like most ancient philosophers, Epicurus aspired to live a happy life. He aimed for peace, fearlessness, and a life that's absent of pain. He proposed a self-sufficient life. I don't agree with all his views, but I like his perspective on pleasure. Pleasure is not only eating, drinking, and being merry—no, true pleasure is to live care-free. But we live our lives far from it. We are always distracted by something. That's why it's difficult to enjoy the moment.

Removing Excessive Desire From Our Lives

Here are a few things many of us want to obtain:

- To live forever

- To have a lot of money

- To be respected

- To have power

- To stay healthy

- To have certain people in our lives

Epicureanism considers these desires as illnesses of the soul. A soul that's pure doesn't want to "obtain" anything. It is complete. It doesn't need anything. It's the same concept that Buddhism and mindfulness propose. And it's a viewpoint we can all benefit from. But how do you practice all these stuff without relying too much on external sources to be happy?

Turns out there's a very simple way that we can be more present. We can stop thinking about the past and the future so we can enjoy the present.

Rely On Your Own Senses

Let's do a little thought exercise. When you walk on the street, take a shower, have a conversation, or sit on a chair, what do you do? Think about it. What happens inside your head when you're doing something?

Almost all of us perform the activity as a secondary thing. Our primary objective is to think. You can easily detect that by looking at how much you rely on your senses on an average day.

Do you FEEL the water on your skin in the shower? Do you HEAR the words someone is saying to you? Do you SEE the buildings you walk by? Do you SMELL the coffee? Do you TASTE the omelet? We all know we have five basic senses. And yet, we're not aware of them. We're only aware of our thoughts. Our thoughts are stealing away our senses. Ever thought about that?

To be more at peace. To enjoy the present. To be less distracted. To be happy…All you need to do is rely more on your senses. Feel, hear, see, smell, and taste life, my friend. It's pretty good. But you already knew that.

"What about my goals?"

At first sight, having goals does not match with living in the present. After all, goals are by definition future oriented. When you set a goal, you aim at something in the future. Is that bad? Like everything in life, nothing is good or bad by itself. We tend to turn our goals into a bad thing by thinking too much about them.

I don't think there's anything wrong with having the intention to make your life better. And if you think about it, all these philosophers, spiritual teachers, and sages all had their goals. They wrote books, started schools, movements, and communities. So when some person tells you goals are bad, walk away.

Start Now

Sometimes we need a reminder to be more present. To enjoy our lives and to make the best of it. Why not increase your awareness right now? Do you feel the device that's in your hand? Do you see the beauty of the place that you're currently in? What do you smell? What do you hear?

Rely on that. And less on your thoughts. You'll find that life will be peaceful. And you'll find that you don't need anything to be happy. Life is good the way it is. You don't need to read another book. You don't need to meditate. You don't NEED anything. It's funny how this awareness removes the worry and stress out of our lives. Because right now, at this moment, there's nothing to worry about. Relying on your senses does that for you. Enjoy!

Summary Of Part I

We covered 10 principles that together form the "work first" mindset. As you can see, it's not complicated. These things are common sense to most of us. But we shouldn't view these things as common sense. We shouldn't take anything for granted. Take anything you do seriously.

In short, the "work first" mindset means that you:

1. Commit to learning and self-improvement
2. Manage your energy
3. Be ambitious
4. Adopt the traits of effective people
5. Rely on yourself
6. Deal with anxiety head-on
7. Let go of things that have a hold on you
8. Break your negative thought loops
9. See things for what they are by adopting Marcus Aurelius' 3 rules for life
10. Be present

Now that we've covered the mindset of highly productive remote work, let's get to the strategy that we can use to actually get more done.

PART II
STRATEGY

'If you spend too much time thinking about a thing, you'll never get it done'

— Bruce Lee

Highly Productive Remote Work Isn't Complicated

I'm all about productivity tools and systems. But sometimes, other writers in this field over-complicate things when it comes to getting things done. They talk about systems that require so much time and energy to follow, that productivity becomes a task by itself. Others are so focused on using the right apps on their phones and computers that they are distracted by technology.

It's easy to miss the mark when it comes to remote work and productivity. Because why do we even use productivity systems? The purpose of productivity is to get things done effectively, so we have more time to spend on things that matter to us. Plus, applying productivity strategies should make doing work more enjoyable.

At least, this is true for most professionals. No one wants to be productive for the sake of being productive. What's the point of that? And no one wants to take all the fun out of their work voluntarily.

If you're reading this book, I bet this is not the first thing you've read about productivity. In fact, the readers of my blog are generally people who've read multiple books on the topic. They know about most of the productivity tips. And yet, they struggle to get things done and feel overwhelmed. This is something I can relate to.

Knowledge itself will not help you to get more done

I can honestly tell you that I've read about every productivity advice that exists. I can never be sure I know *all* tips but in the past 15 years, I've read a lot about how to get more done. Plus, I've *applied* nearly all the advice. I even took cold showers years ago because I read that's supposed to be good. Like most people, I realized that it was a gimmick.

The truth is that *most* advice in this field is a gimmick. People craft all kinds of stories to convince you that their system is the best. I took the opposite approach and often made fun of those types of articles.

That's how a lot of like-minded readers found me. The truth is that mastering productivity is very simple. To get things done, you get in good mental and physical shape. You get your sleep, eat healthy food, avoid alcohol and drugs, and remove distractions from your work environments. Ideally, you also work with a Pomodoro timer to improve your focus.

I'll share the actual productivity tips later in this book. But for now, you don't have to focus on that. All productivity strategies and tips are simple. And yet, it's hard to apply them in daily life. That's why having more knowledge is useless. It will not help you get more done.

We're always in a conflict

Look at this way. You have two voices inside your head. One says, "Screw all this working on your goals stuff. Just kick back and have a little fun." This is especially true for remote work. You're only answering to yourself when you're working remotely. The other voice says, "C'mon, you know that you need to work on yourself. You need to wake up, get your shit together, do you work, hit the gym, eat clean. You'll feel better afterward."

The other voice jumps in, "Afterward!? Screw that! How about *now*!" Those shenanigans go on all day in most of our heads and it will not help you to get things done. When you're constantly managing those voices, you're wasting a lot of energy. Energy that you could be used to read a book, go to the gym, or work on your passion project.

Most of us are aware of this process. As a result, we get frustrated.

At the end of the day, we look back and think, "Why did you eat the whole chocolate bar? And why did I spend all evening on my phone? Was that really necessary?" You and I both know that the answer is no.

The next time you get upset or disappointed if you wasted your time, realize that you have an option. Sometimes we pretend that our focus is outside of our control. After all, there a lot of distractions, even if we're not physically at the office. Emails, Slack messages, annoying co-workers, demanding bosses, useless calls that go on forever, you name it. Don't blame other people for your lack of productivity. You can and you *should* achieve your full potential.

Give this technique a try

It's very simple. Simply sit down or get in the position you work in. *Physically* get in your work position. That's the whole technique.

And that's also the only way to get work done. You know this. But here's the thing. Sometimes we do everything to *avoid* getting into our position. We grab coffee, go for a walk, read a book, run errands, whatever to avoid that chair and desk. I do it all the time. But you know what I also do? I sit myself down. I tell myself, "Do just one thing."

I put my phone away and close my internet browser. Then, I start working on *one small thing* that I scheduled for that day. And then, like magic, I start working. Look, I'm over-simplifying this whole thing. And you're reading a 1000-word chapter on sitting down to get work done. Don't you know this stuff?! Sure you do. So why don't you do it? Honestly, getting things done is sometimes as easy as sitting down.

Guess how I wrote this chapter? Before I sat down, I re-arranged my bookshelf like someone with OCD. I tried to escape. The lazy voice inside my head wanted me to open the Netflix app. But I didn't cave in. *I sat down.*

"Is it really that simple?"

Yes, getting things done is *really* that simple. Now, that doesn't mean staying productive is easy. Making progress in your career and life is difficult. The funny thing is that we only make it more difficult by using the wrong productivity systems.

But at some point, you have to sit down and get started. Put your phone away, grab a cup of coffee/tea, or some water, and get in your working position. Now, just finish *one* task. I tell myself that all the time. And it always works. Don't believe me? Why not try getting in your work position now? Just see what happens next.

Quick Productivity Tips You Can Instantly Apply

Let me share 20 quick tips with you that will make you more productive.

1. Always Cut to The Chase

With everything in life, there's a bunch of crap, and there's stuff that matters. Chit chat, small talk, delaying, waiting around, not speaking up, is all useless. If you want to get shit done, you have to jump straight into the action.

2. Record All Your Thoughts and Ideas

Similar to computers, you have a Random-Access Memory (RAM). Your human RAM stores relevant short-term information. But your RAM capacity is limited. When it's full, older information that you have stored will be deleted to make room for new information. You want to write down your thoughts to unload your RAM, which gives you more brainpower. Even if you never take a look at that note again, it's still worth it.

3. Say No

When it comes to work, I say no to everything that doesn't support my goals and values. We live in an abundant world — there are always enough opportunities.

In my personal life, I say no to everything that doesn't thrill me. When I think 'meh' about something, I always say NO. That eliminates wasting time on shit that I'm not excited about.

4. Take A 5 Minute Break Every 30 To 45 Minutes

This is also called the Pomodoro technique. During the short break, you stretch your back, walk around, or drink some water. But more importantly, you take your nose out of your work. When you come back to your desk, you might have new ideas. Or you might think: "WHAT AM I DOING?" And stop it before you waste all your time.

I use an app for my Mac that displays the timer on my screen. There are a bunch of these Pomodoro apps if you search for them on Google. Any will do.

5. Eliminate Everything That Distracts You

Willpower is overrated. If something distracts you, eliminate it. One of my friends has a news addiction. I suggested to get rid of his tv, delete his news apps, and block the news sites on his laptop. Two weeks later he told me that he's finally starting a business.

Don't think you're immune to your distractions. Remove them.

6. Keep Away Clutter

A cluttered life means a cluttered brain. And with a cluttered brain, you can't get stuff done. I prefer a simple work and living environment.

A desk, a laptop, and a notebook. Keep it simple. You don't need any fluff.

7.   Focus On 1 Thing Some Days

If you have recurring tasks, try to do as much of the same thing on one day. I write 2–3 blog posts on 1 day, the other days of the week I use for my other projects and businesses. On my writing days, I turn off my phone and just write. Nothing else gets in the way.

8.   Stop Consuming So Much Information

You don't need to read 5000 articles on productivity. If you find useful information, try it. Don't search for more. More is not always better. You can only process so much of it. Stop consuming, start creating.

9.   Create Routines

Decisions fatigue your brain. And routines eliminate decisions. Which ultimately means more brainpower. Routines are not OCD — they are efficient. Use them.

10. Don't Multitask

When you juggle multiple things simultaneously, like; sending an email, texting a friend and checking your Facebook while you are in a meeting, you engage in context switching. In a research done by Gloria Mark of the University of California, Irvine, it showed that it takes an average of 25 minutes to return to the original task after an interruption. That's a waste of useful time.

11. Check Email Twice A Day

Every time you check your email, you get a rush of dopamine. I get it — checking email feels nice, and most of us are addicted to it. While dopamine may cause a rush, it also exhausts you. That is why you still feel tired at the end of the day while you have not been productive. To minimize that, turn off notifications, and check your email only twice a day on set times.

12. No Smartphone During the First Hour of Your Day

A smartphone's primary function is to interrupt you. But don't let other people or apps interrupt you during the first hour of your day. Take that first hour to think about the day ahead of you, read a book, enjoy your breakfast, coffee or tea.

13. Plan the Next Day

Every night before I go to bed, I take 5 minutes to set my priorities (usually 3–4) for the next day. That makes me more focused when I wake up. I find that I waste time if I don't do this practice. It's cool to 'go with the flow'. The only problem is I don't want to be a dog that mindlessly chases cars.

14. Keep 'Thinking' To A Minimum

When people say: "I'm thinking." They mean worrying by thinking. Don't think too much. Just DO, and see what happens. If you like what you're seeing, continue. If not, do something else.

15. Exercise

A few things are vital in life: food, water, shelter, relationships, and exercise. Without these things, you can't function properly. Scientific research shows that regular exercise can make you happier, smarter, and more energetic.

16. Laugh A Little

Laughing reduces stress. And if you want to keep up your productivity, you don't want stress. So move the corners of your mouth upward as much as you can.

17. Don't Go to Meetings

This is a tough one for people who work for corporations. Some companies have a 'Meeting' culture. People organize meetings just to look important or procrastinate real work. For goodness sake, PLEASE STOP.

18. Is That Really Necessary?

Ask yourself that question as often as you can. You will find that your answer is often: Nope. So why do unnecessary things?!

19. If You're Having A Shitty Day, Press Reset

You might screw up, maybe someone gets angry with you—shit happens. Don't get down about it. Take some time alone, meditate, listen to music, or go for a walk. Try to get back on track — don't let your day go to waste.

20. Do the Work

Yes, talking about work is easier than doing it. Everyone can talk. But you're not everyone, right? You're a productivity beast. So act like one.

Without these 20 things, I wouldn't be productive at all. You may have noticed that I don't get into details, like which tools and apps I use. I don't think that stuff matters. It's about creating a productivity mindset and environment that let you thrive. I only care about getting things done in a fun and not stressful way. That makes doing work way more fun and rewarding.

Accelerate Your Learning Curve

Accelerated learning is something we should all strive for. But too much advice on the internet promises the impossible:

- "1000X your personal growth!"

- "Change your life in 10 seconds!"

- "Learn EVERYTHING in 1 hour!"

Those things only make us skeptical. That's because you and I both know that these types of claims are BS—it's nothing more than cheap clickbait. But why are we still deceived by these headlines? We're optimists! And there's nothing wrong with that. Look, we all know that there's no such thing as 1,000% growth in a short period of time. We also know that we can't finish a 300-page book in 30 minutes. Mastery doesn't work that way. There are no shortcuts.

However, getting good at something is also not totally unattainable. Because like these above extreme claims, there is a counterculture that says it takes 10,000 hours (or more) to master a skill. As you might expect, I'm more on the side of that it takes longer to get good at something. But I firmly believe there's a difference in the *way* we learn. You can spend 10,000 hours doing something and learn nothing. That's why I'm sharing 5 things that have worked for me in the past to accelerate my learning curve and learn skills faster.

1. Use Best Practices To Accelerate Your Learning

"Don't reinvent the wheel." It's a platitude you often hear. And yet, we all think we're majestic wheel-inventors. When you start learning a skill, it must come from a place of humility and admiration for the practice.

Whether it's writing, value investing, or playing the pan flute; start with the basics. I get that people want to be different and try to do new things. But no one ever started as an "original."

We start by doing what everybody else did. Once you master the basics, you can go out and do your own thing. When I started writing, I copied my favorite authors. And I followed advice from books like On Writing by Stephen King and Ernest Hemingway.

It's the same with investing. I didn't try to create my own strategy from the beginning. I learned about investing from my mentors and from books. I didn't make decisions on my own. That only came later. By listening to best practices, you can avoid making mistakes in the *beginning*. And that's exactly why most people never get good at something. They quit too early. Don't be like most people. Instead, learn from the greats. And have respect for the skill you're learning. That's how you can accelerate your learning curve.

2. Measure And Evaluate Your Progress Weekly

Your goal is to get better at a skill, right? How do you know that you're getting better without measuring it? Measuring your progress is the only way you can evaluate it. You don't need hardcore data to evaluate. I use my journal as an evaluation tool.

Every day, I write about what I've learned. What mistakes I made. What I need to avoid. What I want to focus on. And every week, I review my journal and look at how it went. Did I spend enough time practicing? Did I make enough notes? What should I do differently? That information helps me to evaluate my learning progress.

3. Get Feedback

To accelerate your learning curve, it's important to get input from mentors, coaches, or experts who've done what you're trying to do. I can't stress this enough. Show your progress to an experienced person.

- Play the guitar in front of a teacher

- Send your articles to an established writer

- Discuss your business model with a successful entrepreneur

If you don't have access to an expert, consider paying someone. Getting feedback from a more experienced person is scary. I've been there many times. We don't like to be told that we're doing things wrong. We also don't like to look stupid. That's normal. But what's more important. Your feelings or your career?

Also, good mentors and coaches never make you feel bad. Remember, if they make you feel bad, you've asked the wrong person for advice. Seek out people who are already established and have nothing to prove. They will help you better.

4. Don't Quit

This is so obvious that it often gets left out. You can't master a skill if you quit early. There's no point in talking about that. However, understanding WHY we quit can help us prevent quitting early. So when you're learning a skill, your progress does not grow linearly over time. But we all expect that learning is linear. "The more time I invest in something, the better I should get, right?" Unfortunately, learning skills don't work that way. Our progress looks more like this:

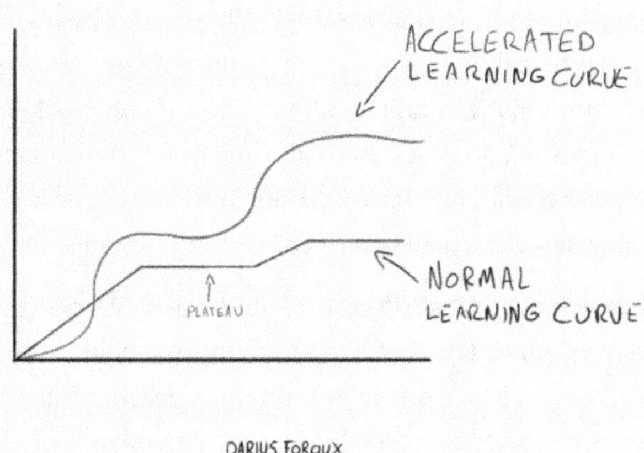

DARIUS FOROUX

We hit learning plateaus—and all of a sudden, we don't get better. But the problem is that time does not stop, only our progress does—and that's very frustrating. And what does frustration cause?

That's right: An urge to quit. So when you stop growing, know why you want to quit. The trick is to acknowledge the urge but not give into it. Remember: When you accelerate your learning curve, you will still hit plateaus (see drawing). The difference is that you expect them. That alone will help you to push through plateaus.

5. Work Harder

"Yeah, but I work smart, dude!" There are always Einsteins who try to tell us that they work "smart." Good for them. But that's not what I'm talking about. Even if you work 2 hours a day. I'm saying: Work hard during those two hours. Every day work hard. Don't hold anything back. That's how you *really* accelerate your learning curve.

I always thought I worked hard. But I wasn't working nearly as hard as I am today. And I can still improve a lot. As you and I both know, hard work is not about appearing busy or doing useless tasks. It has everything to do with *focus*.

I know this sounds cheesy. When you're working, *work*. Don't go for coffee 10 times a day, stop looking at your social media apps, and don't lounge in your chair. Don't wander around, thinking, "what should I do now?" If you want to accelerate your learning, achieve more, and make a contribution, you must take your personal development seriously. You can't slack off. This is not high school.

I'm not always a fan of black/white thinking. But when it comes to getting good at what you do, it is indeed a binary choice: Are you learning or NOT? There's no middle ground. You either move forward, or you go backward. It's up to you.

How To Improve Your Focus

Do you struggle to finish your tasks? Are you always distracted by notifications, gossiping, or anything that's random? In that case, you and I are alike. Because focusing on a single thing is one of the hardest things at work. There's always something that interrupts you, right?

- Another person
- A call
- A meeting
- A false emergency
- Your cat
- A stranger's cat
- News about last night's NBA game

Sure, you can blame those things — but that's weak. You and I both know that those things can't interrupt you without your permission. That means every time you're not focused; you're giving someone or something permission to enter your mind. Scary, isn't it? That's how I look at interruptions. But I have to admit that I can't maintain my focus all the time. Sometimes, I give in. It's not good. Your life doesn't benefit from gossiping, looking at Instagram 439 times a day, watching 49 YouTube videos, and reading negative news articles. So, what can you do to improve your focus? Here are 2 things that I always do when I find myself not being able to focus on what matters.

So, what can you do to improve your focus? Here are 2 things that I always do when I find myself not being able to focus on what matters.

1. Eliminate. Eliminate. Eliminate

Every day, we accumulate stuff. I'm not only talking about the stuff you're buying like clothes, kitchen equipment, house decorations, toys, gadgets, or whatever. We accumulate ideas.

Have you ever thought about that? We're exposed to so many ideas that we adopt some of them, and make them our own. For example, many people have told me to create more YouTube videos. My family, friends, team members, readers, students — everybody has ideas. And they want to help.

Likewise, I also share my ideas with others. Ideas about how you can improve your life, career, business, or relationships. We all do it. And there's nothing wrong with that. It only becomes a problem if you don't filter the input you get from people. So after I heard from people that I should make YouTube videos, I thought to myself "Hey! I should make YouTube videos!"

I've been thinking a lot about that for the past six months. And I also invested a lot of time in creating a strategy. "What should my videos be about? Where should I record them? How should I edit them? What music should I use?" I've been working on it a lot. And I recently published a video as well. The response was positive.

There's only one problem: It consumes too much of my time and attention. As a consequence, I spend less time on writing, podcasting, and creating new courses. And those are exactly the things that I *want* to do. I started a blog for a reason: I love to write, and I'm good at it. Therefore, the work is easier, compared to creating YouTube videos, which I'm not that good at.

Plus, I thoroughly enjoy writing articles, books, and material for my online courses. When the work gets hard, I don't mind. But when I was working on YouTube videos, I got frustrated a lot. And again, my focus and work suffered from it. What did I do when I lacked focus? I asked myself this question:

"What thing(s) should I eliminate to make my life so simple that it's easy to focus?"

In this case, I stopped focusing on YouTube. Elimination is a key strategy that I use for many aspects of my life. We accumulate so much unnecessary baggage throughout the years that we consistently need to eliminate:"What thing(s) should I eliminate to make my life so simple that it's easy to focus?"

In this case, I stopped focusing on YouTube. Elimination is a key strategy that I use for many aspects of my life. We accumulate so much unnecessary baggage throughout the years that we consistently need to eliminate:

- Ideas
- Projects
- Work

- Objects

- And so forth

If you find yourself struggling to focus, try this strategy. Make your life so simple that it's a breeze to live. And let's be honest here. Who wants to live a life that's impossible? Life is already hard enough. Don't make it harder.

2. Think About Past Success

Thinking about past success and happiness stimulates the production of serotonin, a chemical nerve our cells produce. Serotonin is the key chemical that affects every part of your body. Serotonin plays a huge role in our bodily functions. But it also helps to reduce depression, increase libido, stabilize mood, control sleep, and regulate anxiety.

Serotonin also plays a massive role in our general *well-being*. But here's why serotonin matters to your focus. It also regulates delayed gratification. When your serotonin activity goes down, it can lead to a lack of focus on the long-term. You are less likely to act on your plans.

When you lose focus, there's a big chance that your serotonin activity is low. That's why you are giving into short-term pleasures like going out, drinking, shopping, having sex, watching TV, or anything else that gives you short-term pleasure.

To improve your focus, boost your serotonin activity. Research shows that exercise can do that. But something else, that's equally effective, and a lot easier is a simple mind-exercise. All you need to do is remember positive events that happened in the past. Alex Korb, a neuroscientist at UCLA, and the author of The Upward Spiral, explains why remembering positive events help you to focus on what matters:

"All you need to do [to increase serotonin levels] is remember positive events that have happened in your life. This simple act increases serotonin production in the anterior cingulate cortex, which is a region just behind the prefrontal cortex that controls attention."

When serotonin goes up, your focus goes up. Ultimately, that's what you should do.

I know that it sounds cheesy, but when something is wrong, you must fix it. When I can't focus, the first thing I do is to acknowledge that I have a problem that needs a solution. Some people go through life without even acknowledging that they have problems.

- No, it's not normal to check your phone every 2 minutes.

- No, it's not normal to gossip all the time.

- No, it's not normal to be bored.

Focus on your life. Think about what matters to you. Then, do those things and don't get distracted — stay on the path.

How To Stop Wasting Time

The reason I research productivity is simple. I think that a productive life equals a happy life. Also, if you're more productive than average people, you'll advance faster in your career since you learn more and you do more. And eventually rewarded more. And when I talk about productivity, I talk about being effective.

Because productivity doesn't suggest that you get the right things done. It just means that you get a lot of stuff done. But that's not what matters. Effectiveness, however, refers to getting the *right* things done.

And if you want to do your job well, earn money, live a meaningful life, or learn skills, that is what matters the most. Otherwise, you just run around in circles. You might appear busy, but you won't achieve anything meaningful. In other words: It's easy to do useless work. Work that doesn't bring you closer to the outcomes that you desire.

Results matter the most. Practically, that means this: You might work for 50 hours a week, but if you don't experience any growth personally, emotionally, and financially, you're not effective.

People often ask me, "Where do I begin?" To answer that question, I want to share one exercise that I teach in my productivity course: Procrastinate Zero.

It's an exercise that I picked up from Peter Drucker's The Effective Executive. To me, Drucker is the first and best thinker when it comes to effectiveness for knowledge workers.

Many of the books, articles, productivity tools, and productivity apps that you see these days are all in a way influenced by Drucker, who essentially invented the term personal effectiveness. What you will find next is a simple exercise from The Effective Executive (which I modified slightly to make it easier) that you can apply to become more effective yourself.

Step 1: Know Thy Time

I often hear people saying: "I don't know what's wrong with me. I keep procrastinating." My question is: *"Do you know thy time?"*

If you don't measure your time, it's tough to stop procrastination or improve your productivity. Because if you want to manage your time better, you have to know where it goes first. Your memory is not sufficient. If I asked you what you were doing exactly one week ago at this time, would you have an answer? There you go.

How do you know your time? Keep an activity log. Before I even have a real session with clients, I often ask them to keep an activity log for two weeks. An activity log is exactly what you imagine — an hour-by-hour record of what you're doing throughout the day.

The specific method you use for your activity log doesn't matter. The only thing that matters is that you want to keep a record for at least two weeks. Preferably, you want a whole month of recorded activities. I just keep a pen and a notepad on my desk and every hour I write down the time and what I've done during the past hour. It's important to keep the notebook visible, so you don't forget.

Step 2: Identify The Non-Productive Work

This step is actually very simple. I just have one question for you: "Go through all the recurring activities in your log one by one. What would happen if you would stop doing them?"

If the answer is: *"All hell breaks loose."* Don't change anything. But if your answer is: *"Nothing would happen."* You've hit gold. We all do activities that have ZERO return. I call those activities timewasters.

Step 3: Eliminate The Time-Wasters

Boom. That's it. Know where your time goes. Identify the critical tasks from the trivial tasks in your life. And cut the trivial, time-wasting, tasks. *"That simple?"* Yes.

If you want to be a super effective person, you regularly keep a log. You don't have to keep a log for 365 days a year. Instead, do two stretches of two-three weeks a year. That's enough to keep track of your time and identify new timewasters.

Also, the additional benefit of such a simple exercise is that it forces you to think about your daily routine. Often, we start time-wasting activities, and they become habits. And if you don't become aware of the pointless behavior, it's difficult to break those bad habits. I've found this exercise to be one of the most powerful things in productivity. Start now. Your activity log probably looks something like this:

- (insert time) — Read Darius Foroux' chapter about keeping a time-log and started my own time-log.

- (insert time) — Turned off my phone and got back to (whatever you were working on).

- (insert time) — Browsed the news, Facebook, Instagram, and watched YouTube videos. (Be honest with yourself. Shit happens).

- (insert time) — Responded to emails.

Great. I'm happy to see that you started. Now keep going for another two weeks.

Take A Vacation

You recharge your phone when it runs out of juice. You refill your gas tank when you're running on empty. But sometimes, you forget to take a break and recharge your most precious possession: Your body (and the brain that's inside of it).

Whether you love what you do, are in between jobs, or have a job you hate: You're working. *Living* is also a job. A pretty tough one, actually. Just the act of getting up in the morning can be a daunting task. And I'm not even talking about all the responsibilities we have.

So why do you make your life even more challenging by not taking a vacation to recharge? I'm not talking about your weekends that are packed with activities, or holidays where you do more work than relax. No, that type of "free time" only *costs* energy. I'm talking about resting with a very specific reason: To recharge your battery so you can get back to living a productive life.

A break reduces stress and improves productivity.

Scientific research shows that a vacation decreases perceived job stress and burnout. Now, that's a pretty solid benefit of taking a few days off. But there's more. As you may know, I'm always interested in productivity. In the case of resting or a vacation, my question is: **Will I get more things done when I get back?**

The answer is yes, but there's one major thing to keep in mind. But let's back up a bit: What does it mean to get more done? Getting things done has nothing to do with time—if you work more hours— you don't necessarily get more done. In fact, research shows that working more hours generally means less productivity.

Why? Well, we often waste time if we have a lot of it. It's simple: If I say to you, you have a year to write an article. What would you do? Put it off until tomorrow, right?

But what if I tell you that you only have 2 hours? You'll probably get started right away. So in a way, having more days off, and fewer days to work, forces you to be more effective with your time. Research shows that a vacation in itself won't make you more productive, but when you have more days off, you have a strong desire to get more things done in less time.

And that's a win-win situation for everybody: You, your business, or your job. You take off a few days, recharge, spend time with your family or friends, and when you come back, you're more productive. Sounds great. But wait, there's a caveat. When your vacation is stressful, the positive benefits go away. So keep the stress at a minimum on your holiday. Otherwise, you've wasted a perfect opportunity to relax and boost your overall productivity.

I recently felt I needed a break for several reasons. I had a few injuries that didn't seem to go away and had less energy. I could have powered through, but instead, I decided to go on a vacation with my family. For a week, I did absolutely no work. And when I came back, I was full of energy. Here are a few tips that might help you to take a break that fully recharges you.

1. Do What You Want

There are no rules for taking vacations and everybody relaxes in a different way. If you like to plan your holiday, just do it. If you want to go with the flow, then do that. Want to wake up early? Do it. Don't like waking up early? Sleep in. Even if you go on a vacation with your partner, friends, or family, you don't have to be together 24/7. You can also sometimes do things that *you* enjoy.

The key is to not have expectations on your vacation. Let go of everything. I also don't like to post vacation pictures on social media. Otherwise, I'm constantly thinking about taking a cool picture so I can impress others.

You'll probably even do things you wouldn't do just to take a picture. "I really need to rent a jet ski so I can take a picture with it." No, you don't. Who cares? Focus on enjoying the moments you experience. *Whatever* those moments may be.

2. Read

Bill Gates is famous for his voracious reading habit. He is also known for his 'Think Week' where he does nothing else but read and think. You don't have to be Bill Gates to think about your life and career. We all have our daily, weekly, and monthly routines. Usually, routines and habits work very well. However, you can also get stuck inside a loop.

That's why I recommend you to step back from your daily life and career. If you do that, two things can happen: When you step away, you miss your daily life and can't wait to pick up where you left off. Or the opposite will happen: You *don't* want to go back. See that as a sign that you need to make a change. Either way, a break always serves a purpose. It doesn't only help you to recharge, it will also make you think. That's why I like to read for hours on my vacation.

3. Get Bored

One of my favorite strategies for finding new ideas is to get bored out of my mind. It sounds easier than it is because of distractions. In the past, I would do everything to NOT get bored: Watch TV, go out, browse Facebook, etc. But did you know that you can use boredom to your advantage? Instead of giving into distractions, just give into the boredom and see where it leads your mind to.

In fact, one of my favorite artists of all time, Andy Warhol, embraced boredom. You can tell by the boring films he made or the references he made in his book The Philosophy of Andy Warhol about getting bored.

Whenever I hit a creative wall, I just do nothing. Literally, nothing. Try it sometimes. It's a great strategy; maybe you come up with the next best thing in your industry. It's never a good time to take a break.

- "I just need to finish this project."

- "My boss will never accept it."

- "People will think I'm lazy."

- "I don't have time."

- "My family needs me."

Yeah, yeah, I've been there too. But what would you rather: Continue to work without resting and burn out? Or take some rest before you're tired? So before you use all those valid reasons to *not* take a break, think about what all the people in your life have to do if you're not here anymore. Yes, you're important. So take care of yourself. Take a break and come back with more energy.

The Busyness Trap

Do you know that feeling of being so busy that time flies with a blink of an eye? We're so busy with all kinds of things—work, friends, going out, holidays, etc. But being busy is not a good thing at all.

Especially because we waste most of our time on nonsense. We say we're busy but in reality, we just fill up our lives with crap. We binge-watch tv shows for days, we go to networking events with weirdos who try to sell you their services, we spend hours finding new clothes to buy so we can impress people we don't even like.

We're busy with bullshit. But until a few years ago, I never got it. When people asked me, "how are you," my answer was, "busy." What's wrong with us? Why are we so busy with things that don't matter?

We even use our busyness as an excuse for important things. That's sad. After I realized that I wasn't in control of my life, I decided to stop being busy. Being busy is an excuse that losers use. I say that because you can use "busy" as an excuse for everything.

- **You forgot your anniversary.** "Yeah, but you know how busy I am, right? I'll make it up to you."

- You haven't called your mother in six months. "Mom, I'm sooo busy."

- **You didn't go to the gym.** "I'm too busy to work out."

- **And the WORST:** "I'm too busy to work on the stuff that makes me happy." That can be your music, business, model trains, or whatever.

I've used all those excuses. But at some point, I told myself this: How on earth can you be too busy to give someone that's important to you a call? That's nonsense. Every time you say you're busy, you're actually saying that you can't prioritize your life. Most people identify being busy with being successful. But unlike 95% of the people I know, I don't think being busy means that you're successful.

When you meet people, they often want to show you that they have busy lives. "A full calendar must mean that I'm doing SOMETHING right, right?" The truth is: If you're busy, you don't live at all. You just exist. Derek Sivers, author of Anything You Want, and one of my favorite thinkers, says: *"To me, 'busy' implies that the person is out of control of their life."*

"But if I'm not busy, what the hell should I do?"

Slow down there. Take a step back. And think about which things in your life are just 'busy work' and not meaningful. Seneca put it best:

"A good man will not waste himself upon mean and discreditable work or be busy merely for the sake of being busy."

Here's how I put that in practice. It's absolutely fine if you DON'T have plans for the weekend. People's favorite question on Monday is: "What did you do over the weekend?" You don't have to do things so you can tell others about it. If people ask me, this is what I say: "NOTHING." Or, I say: "I wrote, went to the gym, and had dinner with family." And they look at me like: "That's all?" What? I'm not cool if I didn't travel the world, had dinner with aboriginals, and jumped out of a jumbo jet on the way back?

Another thing: I say NO a lot.

Want to grab coffee all day? Want to write an article for money? Want to work for us? Want to do this, or that? No, not now—I don't want to be busy. It's a trap.

When you're busy, time moves fast. And I want time to move SLOW. That's why I only say yes to things that matter to me. You know that feeling? Some days seem like forever, and years later, you still remember how you felt that day. You should feel like that almost every day. All you have to do is slow down, stop being busy, don't forget about important things, and live a conscious life. It's not that difficult, right? You can start now.

15 Useful Things You Can Do With Your Time

Our time on this planet is limited. Most of us realize that sooner or later. And yet, we keep on squandering our time and running around in circles. Why is it that we waste so much of our time? Most people think that we, humans, don't understand the value of time.

I don't think that's the problem. You and I both know the value of time. It's a depletable resource. By that definition, the value of time is high. So if the problem is not our appreciation of time, what's the cause of a waste of time and potential? The answer is obvious: We simply don't know what to do with our time. Seneca, a Roman Stoic Philosopher, famously said in On the Shortness of Life: *"It is not that we have a short time to live, but that we waste a lot of it."* Most of us read that and get a temporary boost: "Wow, I need to value my time and stop wasting it."

You know what we do next? We open Instagram and waste 42 minutes on consuming *shit*. We go out for coffee for the *7th* time this week. We play video games for 2 hours *straight*. We gossip on the phone for *55* minutes.

Ask yourself: Are the things that I'm doing *worth* my time? I've done that. And most of the things that I did simply were not. But distinguishing wasteful activities from worthwhile activities is hard. As an exercise, I recommend everyone to sit down and think about *what* activities are worth your time. This is a personal exercise. Everybody values different things. To give you an idea of how I spend my time, I've made a list of 15 activities that I consider worthwhile.

1. **Working out** — I especially like strength training because being strong is one of the most useful things in life. Sitting behind your desk for hours, going shopping, traveling — your life will be a lot easier when you're physically strong.

2. **Spending time with people you love** — It doesn't really matter what you do. It's more about being around people you genuinely care about. That will lift your spirits and give you energy.

3. **Learning how your body works** — Everybody should know how their body functions. I also like to read about the latest scientific research about health and fitness.

4. **Journaling** — It's always nice to sit down at the end of a day and reflect. What did I do today? What did I learn? What am I going to do tomorrow? Answering those questions is the best time you'll spend every day.

5. **Learning a skill** — Always be learning a new skill. I started practicing Brazilian Jiu-Jitsu a while back. I go to class every week and I constantly learn from YouTube videos. I always want to learn a new skill because it reminds me that I'm always a student.

6. **Making a financial strategy** — I like to read and hear about investing strategies of different people. Even though I consider myself a value investor, I still look at what day traders do. I'm interested in finance because I don't want to waste my hard-earned money.

7. **Watching good movies/tv shows** — I sometimes make fun of people who binge watch tv shows. I think that's a waste of your day. But I love movies and good shows. They can give you inspiration too.

8. **Listening to music** — I listen to music a lot. It gives me inspiration and energy. The best thing is to listen music that fits your mood.

9. **Reading** — I start and close my day with reading. And I never miss a day.

10. **Talking about life** — It's nice to have a good conversation with someone who has the same mindset as you. I've grown to hate shallow conversations. So I don't waste my time anymore on people who I don't have a deep connection with.

11. **Going to the sauna** — I do this twice a week. It's apparently good for you. But that's not why I go. I love the heat and quiet. The time I spend in the sauna is like meditation to me.

12. **Discovering new books** — I can spend hours browsing books that I want to read. But I try to not overdo it. Otherwise, you're reading more ABOUT books than reading actual books.

13. **Watching sport**s — I used to play basketball and I still enjoy watching it. But I only follow the NBA, not all professional sports.

14. **Laughing** — I love some good banter. Life is hard and if you don't laugh about yourself, you only make it harder.

15. **Working on your goals** — Every minute you spend on advancing your life is time you don't regret spending.

At the end of a day, you must look back and tell yourself, "If this was my last day, I'm okay with that." Can you honestly say that? Look, it's not about living every day like it's your last. If everybody did that, we would have total anarchy. Instead, make sure that you spend your time well. Are you proud of how you're spending your days? Answer yes, and you'll never live with regrets.

How To Stay Productive During Chaos

In a perfect world, everything is steady. You can make plans that actually come true 100% of the time. You can anticipate things in advance. But as you and I both know, that's not how life works. In real life, a single random (and unexpected) event can suddenly screw up all your plans, goals, and good intentions to make a change. Think of...

- A family member passes away.

- Getting pregnant.

- Getting into a car accident.

- A calamity at work that causes bankruptcy.

These are individual strategies. But we also have to deal with natural disasters, wars, pandemics, you name it.

Unplanned events can disrupt everything. I've experienced that several times in my life. And there's nothing you can do to prevent unexpected events. Life can be unpredictable. And despite that unpredictability, we still have to function. We must wake up, treat the people in our lives with respect, do our work, and find inner calm. The way I see it, we have two choices.

1. We accept that life is chaos and find a way to adapt ourselves.

2. We refuse to adapt and become miserable because "life is hard."

To me, it's a no-brainer. I choose the former. But how do you adapt when life is uncertain? How do you still manage to be productive when you can't even catch your breath before you have to deal with the next thing? Here are 3 tips that can help you with those challenges.

1. Stay focused on your tasks

When something important interrupts your life, it's easy to develop tunnel vision. Before you know it, your whole life can be consumed by something random. Let's say there's a public health crisis going on in the world. We need to monitor the situation. But we can't allow ourselves to forget where we are going in life. We can't neglect our work, family, friends, and health—under any circumstances.

To stay focused and not give up my ideals, I keep reminding myself of why I do what I do. I do that through daily journaling. No matter how hectic your life is, you can always find 10 minutes to sit down and reflect. No excuses. Plus, I keep looking at my goals almost every day. That reminds me of where I want to go. And when you know where you want to go, you'll keep going. It's as simple as that.

2. Work in short bursts

Always be prepared to get work done. Every time you have a moment to yourself, don't play with your phone, but instead, squeeze in some work. Even if it's only 8 minutes. I bring my laptop and notebook with me wherever I go. Those two things are always by my side. When my life lacks structure, I whip out the laptop at any free moment I have.

Doesn't matter what time it is, where I am, or how long I can work—when I get the chance, *I work.* But working in short bursts is not that easy. After all, you can't truly focus. In a perfect world, you have hours of time blocked for a single important task. That's how you do deep work.

Working in short bursts *only* works if you know what you have to do (Step 1). That's why I always keep a long list of things that I have to do. So when I work in short bursts, I know that I can't waste my time browsing the internet or thinking, "What should I do next?" The process is simple. I grab my laptop, look at my list, and pick one thing that I feel like doing at that time. My list consists of essential tasks. So it doesn't matter which task gets done first.

For example, this is about the ninth time (I lost count) I'm working on this piece. My life has no structure right now. But that's okay. I still write my articles. Remember: Your goal is not to work like this is forever. When you've weathered the storm, get back to your regular routines.

3. Fuel yourself

Life can be demanding. You need proper fuel to handle the physical and mental stress that you endure. I'm no diet expert. But I am an expert on *my* personal diet. Usually, I'm not a fan of trial and error. But when it comes to dieting, it's my go-to strategy.

I've tried many different diets and eating patterns. I currently eat mostly protein and unsaturated fat as my first meal, which is around 11:30am. In other words, I skip breakfast. That's what they call intermittent fasting these days. There's nothing new about that. People have been skipping breakfast for ages. Look, I can't give you diet recommendations because it's different for every person. But I can share a few things you should consider:

- Don't believe everything you read from the health industry. Everybody has something to sell (I'm not only talking about products, but also ideas).

- Distinguish the difference between eating patterns (when you eat, how often, etc.) and diets (the type of foods you consume like protein, fat, carbs).

- Be careful with experimentation. Only try things that are NOT harmful to your body (don't starve yourself, don't try weird diets like eating red meat only).

- Keep notes on how you feel after what food you eat. Exclude things from your diet that make you feel bad.Don't believe everything you read from the health industry. Everybody has something to sell (I'm not only talking about products, but also ideas).

- Distinguish the difference between eating patterns (when you eat, how often, etc.) and diets (the type of foods you consume like protein, fat, carbs).

- Be careful with experimentation. Only try things that are NOT harmful to your body (don't starve yourself, don't try weird diets like eating red meat only).

- Keep notes on how you feel after what food you eat. Exclude things from your diet that make you feel bad.

That's how I've found the ideal foods and eating pattern for me. For example, I eat rice every evening. I love it. Without eating rice, I get hungry very quickly and don't feel as sharp. Should I stop eating rice because some random internet person says so? No, of course not.

Finding Structure In Chaos

In the past, I hated uncertainty. I think that's something you learn as you grow up. "Get a safe job!" is what people say. But they don't tell you that a safe job will ultimately make you lazy and weak. Why? Because you're *safe*. It's counterintuitive, but the reality is that uncertainty forces action. That's why I've grown to love uncertainty. It forces me to find solutions to every challenge I face. And once you live your life that way, you can't even function properly without challenges. When you've reached that stage, know that you're *actually* safe.

Unproductive Habits You Want To Quit

The reason I study productivity is because I'm an unproductive person. I truly am. I sleep too much. I talk too much. I read too much. I listen to music all day. I watch movies. I buy gadgets that turn me into a zombie.

If it wasn't for my productivity system, I wouldn't get anything done. I wouldn't even write this piece. But if you browse social media, all you see is super productive, healthy, and wealthy people. Is that really the case? I don't know. I just know this: You can't be productive 24/7. And a big part of being productive is about getting rid of unproductive habits that we all have.

What follows is a list of eleven unproductive habits that I learned to do less or eliminate. Do you have a few of these habits? Don't worry, we're all unproductive at times. But if you have five or more, it might be time to change. Let's start.

1. Overworking

Some days I can work for 12 or 13 hours straight. I just take a break for exercising and eating. And I can keep that up for a few days. But after a few days, there always comes a crash. Big time. I struggle. I can't get stuff done. I don't even want to get stuff done. It's not good. So I learned to be more calculated with how much I work. Like Ernest Hemingway, stop working at the height of your day.

2. Worrying

What if I go broke? What if I lose my job? What if she doesn't love me? What if I get cancer? What if this plane crashes? What if I lose my sight? What if I...? You got your head so far in the sand like an ostrich that you can't see how self-absorbed that way of thinking is.

Here's the thing: YOU'RE NOT GOING TO DIE RIGHT THIS SECOND. Get over yourself. Stop worrying. And do something useful.

3. Stubbornness

We deal with people all the time. Do you ever think: "Why should I listen to this guy?" Or: "What does she know?" I don't know. Maybe more than you do? We just don't know until we listen to others. When you're always cynical and stubborn, you're actually sabotaging yourself.

4. Ignoring Your Health

The way you feel determines the quality of your work. If you're always tired and feel bad, how do you expect to do great work? When you're in good shape and eat well, your work will reflect that.

5. Checking Things

What are you doing? We often say something like "I was just checking Instagram," or something like that. But "checking" is not a useful activity.

It might be a verb, but it's not a real action. When I started blogging, I always checked my stats for no reason. Then I thought: What's the outcome of checking? Nothing. So stop doing it.

6.   Not Having Goals

Every time successful people say, "I don't have goals," I know that they are full of shit. Who can be successful at anything without aiming for it? Don't believe the stories. People just want to make you believe they became successful without effort. Set a goal, and then work towards it.

7.   Saying Yes

Most people are afraid to say no. Maybe you don't want to let people down. Maybe you're uncomfortable with the word no. I don't know. Doesn't matter, really. What matters is this: If you keep saying yes, you're living someone else's life. Think about it. Deep down, we all know that it's true. We're not even in control of our own time. Want to be in full control of your life? Say no to a million things and yes to a few things that matter.

8.   Relying on Your Memory

Not writing down your thoughts, ideas, tasks, etc., is insane. Why? Because you're wasting a lot of brain power when you rely on your memory. When you write everything down, you can use your brainpower for other things. Like solving problems. That's actually useful and advances your career.

9. Neglecting Your Personal Education

"Woohoo! I finished college. Goodbye lame old books!" Who learns one thing and stops forever? I don't even know why we have that idea planted in our brain. I always thought that learning stops when you get out of school. But the truth is: Your life stops when learning stops. Invest in yourself. Learn something. Read books. Get courses. Watch videos. Do it from home or go places. It doesn't matter. Just learn new things. You'll be more productive and more excited about life.

10. Complaining

We all know, and yet, we all do it. Complaining is one of those habits we always try to quit. But it never lasts. I'm no different. That's why I always remind myself that complaining is a waste of effort. Just the awareness of that will help you to stop.

11. Lack of Focus

Many successful people say that the ability to focus is the number one reason they've made it big. And it's no surprise. The people who are all over the place never seem to get anywhere.

Often, people don't understand why I focus on what *not* to do. The reason is that I like to learn by inverting. It's the same strategy Warren Buffett and Charlie Munger used to become two of the most well-known investors in the world.

When you want to become successful or productive, look at how you become the opposite. Turn things upside down. That's what we've done in this chapter. By simply avoiding these unproductive habits, you'll automatically become more productive. When you combine this with a handful of productivity tips you have a reliable system.

And I always rely on my system to work smarter, better, happier, and effectively. It took me years to figure out that having a system is a good thing, and a few more years to create one, but it was worth it. Because now, I get to be a productive person. Not bad for an unproductive person, right?

Summary Of Part II

We're at the end. I hope you have enough tools for highly productive remote work. As you've seen, it's not complicated. We could have spent hours and hours on explaining all the productivity tips in the world. But ultimately, we must do the work. In short, highly productive remote work means that you:

1. Get in the working position every day...and get to work.

2. Accelerate your learning curve so you learn faster

3. Eliminate distractions to stay focused

4. Keep an activity log and remove time-wasting activities

5. Take time off before you're tired

6. Avoid the busyness trap

7. Say no to things that don't give you energy

8. Spend your time in a useful way

9. Keep going even when there's chaos in your life

10. Avoid the habits of unproductive people

Ultimately, we must find a balance between focusing on what we control (ourselves) and what we don't (everything else). That's not an easy process. But look at it as a challenge. Find a way to be productive from home and be mindful of your surroundings. And while you're working remotely, don't forget to enjoy it too. You decide what to do next. Doesn't that feel good?

Thank You

It means a lot to me that you read this book until the end. I hope you found the ideas useful. If you did, and want to help spreading the word, consider doing one of the following things:

- Talk about freedom with your family, friends, co-workers, or on social media

- Inspire others to be free

- Write a review on Amazon

- Buy the paperback for your family, friends, or team

Or anything else you think will help. I'm not asking you to support this book because I'm an independent writer. In fact, I take pride in the fact that the only person I have to answer to is you, my reader.

I don't answer to a publisher, editor or agent. I'm not the type who listens to people who don't have the same intentions as I. I'm here to help others and share the truth. That's why I self-publish my work. I want to be in control. I only listen to my readers. And my readers are the only people who support me.

For that, I say thank you.

If you want to stay in touch or write me an email, sign up to my free newsletter here: http://dariusforoux.com.

-Darius

About The Author

Darius Foroux (1987) is the author of 7 books. Since 2015, he's sharing his thoughts about life, business, and productivity on my blog. He also co-founded Vartex, a laundry technology company, while he was finishing his master's degree in Marketing in 2010. For his podcast, The Darius Foroux Show, he's interviewed thought leaders like Ryan Holiday, Cal Newport, Robert Sutton, Jimmy Soni, and more. More books by Darius Foroux:

- Win Your Inner Battles (2016)
- How To Go From Procrastinate Hero to Procrastinate Zero (2016)
- THINK STRAIGHT (2017)
- Do It Today (2018)
- The Road To Better Habits (2019)
- What It Takes To Be Free (2019)

Learn more on http://dariusforoux.com/books.